The Life Cycle of a

FROG

John Williams

Illustrated by
Jackie Harland

Reading Consultant:
Diana Bentley

The Bookwright Press
New York · 1988

First published in the
United States in 1988 by
The Bookwright Press
387 Park Avenue South
New York, NY 10016

First published in 1987 by
Wayland (Publishers) Limited
61 Western Road, Hove
East Sussex, BN3 1JD, England

ISBN 0-531-18161-X

Library of Congress Catalog Card Number: 87-71472

Typeset in the UK by DP Press Limited, Sevenoaks, Kent
Printed by Casterman S.A., Belgium

Contents

All the words that are
in **bold** are explained in
the glossary on page 31.

The story of a frog

Here are two adult frogs in a pond. Did you know that frogs can live on the land and in the water? A frog is a kind of animal called an **amphibian**. An amphibian always begins its life in water.

The female lays her eggs

The male frog holds the female to **mate** with her. As she lays the eggs he covers them with a liquid from his body. The liquid is called **sperm**. Now the eggs can begin to grow. They stick together and we call this **frogspawn**.

The eggs grow

The frogspawn floats on the top of the pond. Soon the eggs start to change shape. After seven days they have almost changed into **tadpoles**. Can you see how the head and tail have grown inside the jelly ball?

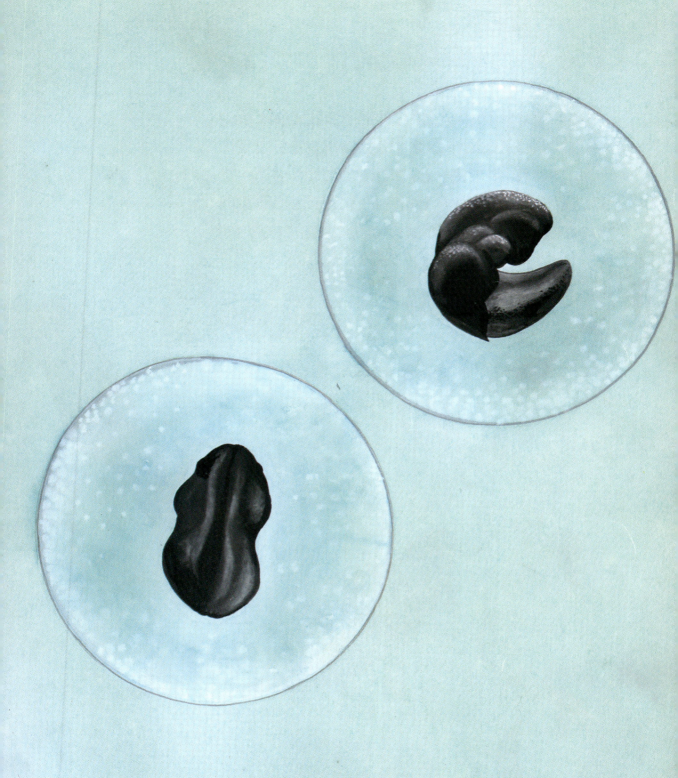

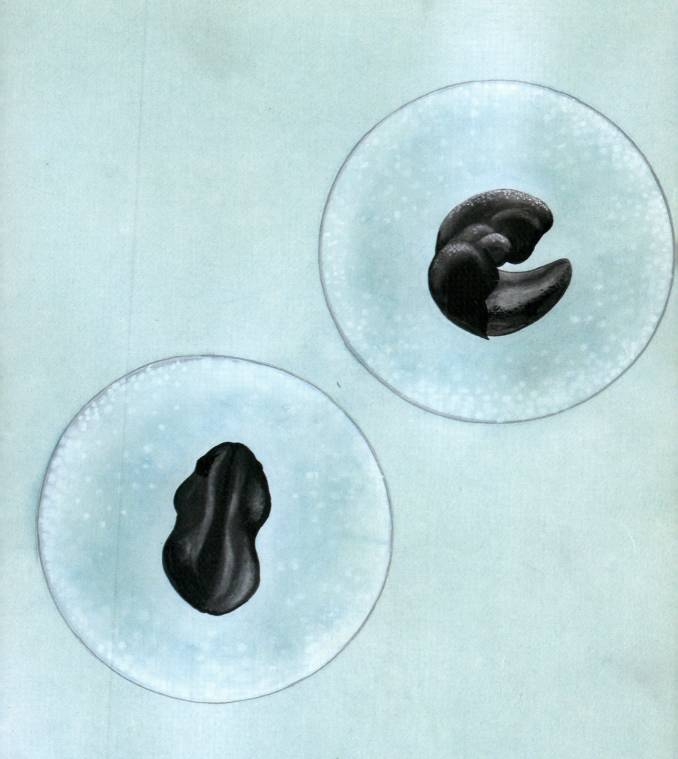

The tadpoles hatch

After about ten days the tadpoles are ready to **hatch** out. They wiggle and wiggle until they are out of the jelly balls. Only a few will live long enough to become frogs. Many are eaten by fish.

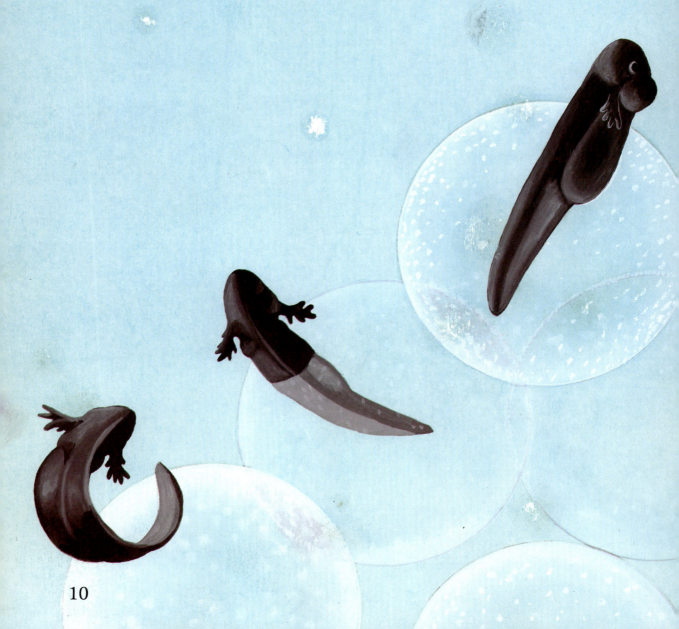

12

The tadpoles swim

Can you see the feathery things on each side of the tadpole's head? These are called the **gills**. Tadpoles need gills so that they can **breathe** under the water.

14

How tadpoles grow

When tadpoles are very young they eat small water plants. As they grow bigger they can eat small water animals. The tadpoles still have their gills but now they are tucked inside the skin.

The tadpoles grow hind legs

At last the tadpoles begin to grow hind legs. It is seven weeks since they hatched from their eggs. They have also grown **lungs** inside their bodies. Now they have to come up to the surface and breathe the air through their mouths.

The back legs grow bigger

The tadpoles still need their tails to swim. The front legs are now growing under the skin where the gills used to be. Can you see the bulges where the front legs are growing?

The tadpoles have four legs

Look at these two tadpoles. It is twelve weeks since they hatched. They have four legs. They will soon start to use them. Only the back ones are used for swimming. Can you see the long toes on the back feet?

The tail disappears

Look again. The tadpole's tail is getting shorter. Can you see the **webs** between the toes on the back feet? These help the frog to swim quickly.

24

The young frogs leave the pond

Young frogs are called froglets. Of course they are very tiny – only about the size of a thimble! They begin to look for food. They use their long sticky tongues to catch insects and tiny animals.

The tiny frogs grow up

Slowly, the frogs grow up to look like their parents. After three years the females will lay their eggs in a pond. What do you think will happen then?

Keeping tadpoles

Only collect from ponds that have a lot
of frogspawn. Do not put tadpoles in
new tap water. Leave the water in a
tank for two days. Put clean sand and
stones in the tank. Remember, one large
stone must be higher than the water.
Put in fresh water plants and a water
snail. These will keep the water clean.

When they are very small tadpoles will eat the plants. When they grow bigger they will eat meat. Hang a small piece of meat in the water. Do not keep it there long because it will make the water dirty. When they have grown front legs they will climb out of the water. Now return them to their pond.

The life cycle of a frog

How many stages of the life cycle can you remember?

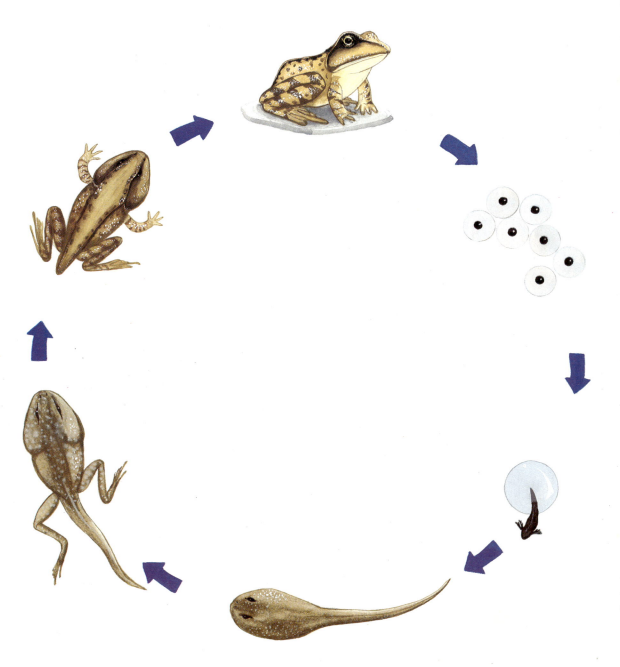

Glossary

Amphibian An animal that starts life in water but later can move on land. Some, like frogs, will grow up and spend a lot of time on the land.

Breathe To take fresh air into the body and to give stale air out. All animals need air to live.

Frogspawn The hundreds of growing eggs are called frogspawn. They stick together and float to the top of the pond.

Gills All animals that breathe under water need gills. Gills help them take air from the water.

Hatch To break out of an egg.

Lungs Animals that breathe air as we do need lungs. Lungs are air bags inside the body of the animal.

Mate To join as a male (father) and female (mother) in order to have babies.

Sperm This is the liquid from the male frog that mixes with the female's eggs. If this does not happen the eggs will not grow into young frogs.

Tadpoles These are the little animals that hatch out of the frog's eggs.

Webs These are pieces of skin stretched between the toes. They help in swimming.

Finding out more

Here are some books to read to find out more.

Amphibians as Pets by George and Lisbeth Zappler.
Doubleday, 1973.
Frogs and Toads by Jane Dallinger and Sylvia A.
Johnson. Dodd, 1975.
Frogs and Toads of the World by Hilda Simon. Lippincott
Jr. Books, 1975.
Peeper, First Voice of Spring, by Robert M. McClung.
Morrow, 1977.

Index

21